the

of the Automobile Industry.

By

Carlos Segura

TROPE PUBLISHING Co.

CARLOS SEGURA

A	is for Azzurra.
B	is for Bentley.
C	is for Cruise.
D	is for Daihatsu.
E	is for Elizalde.
F	is for Farman.
G	is for Gilco.
H	is for Horch.
I	is for I by BMW.
J	is for Jensen.
K	is for Kaiser-Frazer.
L	is for Leon Laisne.
M	is for Mors.
N	is for N by Hyundai.
O	is for Opel.
P	is for Piaggio.
Q	is for Qoros.
R	is for Rolls-Royce.
S	is for Studebaker.
T	is for Tucker.
U	is for Unimog.
V	is for Voltra.
W	is for Wolseley.
X	is for X by AMC.
Y	is for Yugo.
Z	is for Zagato.

A IS FOR AZZURRA

Created in 1966 and marketed by Fiat, the Pininfarina Fiat Spider Azzurra became one of the company's most successful designs.

After being retired by Fiat, Pininfarina continued production of the 124 Sport Spider for the North American market from 1982-1985, using the name Pininfarina Spider Azzurra.

Fiat and Pininfarina are from Italy.

B IS FOR BENTLEY

Bentley was founded in 1919 by mechanical engineer and racing driver Walter Owen Bentley.

Bentley's first model, EXP2, won its first racing event at England's Brooklands track when driver Frank Clement claimed victory in 1921.

Bentley is from England.

C IS FOR CRUISE

Cruise was founded in 2013 by Kyle Vogt and Dan Kan with the aim of making the dream of self-driving cars a reality.

Cruise was acquired by General Motors in 2016 and is now the autonomous vehicle division of the company.

Cruise is from the USA.

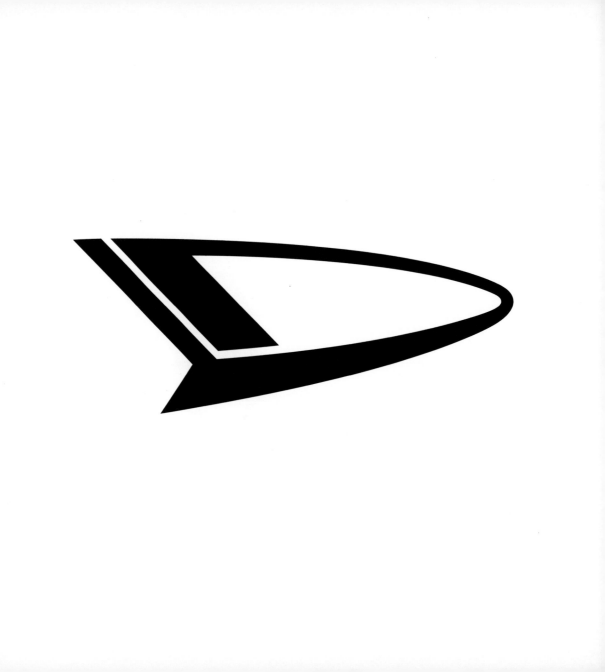

D IS FOR DAIHATSU

Founded in 1907 as the Hatsudoki Seizo Company,
it was renamed Daihatsu in 1951.

Historically known for manufacturing 3-wheeled and
off-road vehicles, Daihatsu now specializes in compact
cars known as kei jidosha in Japan.

Daihatsu is from Japan.

E IS FOR ELIZALDE

Founded by Arturo Elizalde Rouvier in 1915, Elizalde was a Barcelona-based automobile manufacturer that produced cars until 1928.

In 1915, King Alfonso XIII of Spain commissioned the manufacture of an Elizalde Type 20 cabriolet for his personal use.

Elizalde is from Spain.

F IS FOR FARMAN

Farman rose to fame during WWI, not due to their cars, but because their aircraft were exported all over the world.

Its powerful engine reflected the slogan "a car runs, a Farman glides." Despite being regarded as one of the world's finest luxury cars, only about 120 were ever built.

Farman is from France.

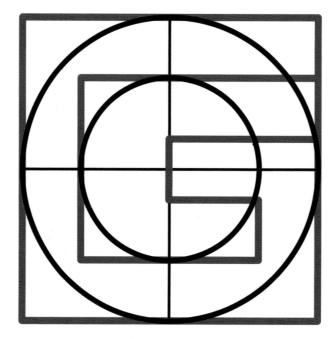

G IS FOR GILCO

Gilco was started by Gilberto Colombo in the early 1940s specifically to produce ultra-light frames for cars.

Enzo Ferrari used Gilco frames for the Ferrari F1.

Gilco is from Italy.

H IS FOR HORCH

One of the pioneering figures of Germany's automotive industry, August Horch founded the Horch & Cie motor vehicle company in 1899.

10 years later, he left the company he founded to start a new company. He came up with the name for this new company by translating his name, which means "hark!; listen!," into Latin: Audi.

Horch is from Germany.

I IS FOR I by BMW

Launched in 2011, the BMWi was founded to design and manufacture plug-in electric vehicles.

The first cars produced for the brand were the BMW i3 and BMW i8.

BMWi is from Germany.

IS FOR JENSEN

Jensen Motors Limited was founded by brothers and body stylists Alan and Richard Jensen.

In 1934, Clark Gable commissioned Jensen to design and build a car for him based on a Ford V8 frame.

Jensen is from England.

K IS FOR KAISER-FRAZER

Kaiser-Frazer was founded by Henry J. Kaiser
and Joseph W. Frazer in 1945.

Kaiser-Frazer introduced the first hatchbacks to the
US market with their Traveler and Vagabond models.

Kaiser-Frazer is from the USA.

L IS FOR LEON LAISNE

Founded in 1913, Leon Laisne was well-known for their design, but they never achieved commercial success.

Englishman Murray Harris joined the company in 1926, changing the company's name to Harris Leon Laisne.

Leon Laisne is from France.

PAGES 26-27

M IS FOR MORS

Founded by Emile Mors in 1895, the Mors automobile was a pioneer of the industry.

Mors was one of the first car manufacturers to participate in automobile racing, beginning in 1897.

Mors is from France.

N IS FOR N by HYUNDAI

Hyundai's N sub-brand of high-performance cars was established in 2012.

The N brand takes its name from Namyang, the district in South Korea where the brand was founded, and the Nürburgring racetrack in Germany where N models are tested. The N logo design was inspired by the curves of a racetrack.

Hyundai "N" is from South Korea

O IS FOR OPEL

Founded by Adam Opel in 1862, the company initially produced only sewing machines, but began to sell high-wheel bicycles, also known as penny-farthings, in 1886. At the time of Adam Opel's death in 1895, the company was the leader in both markets.

Adam's widow and two sons partnered with Friedrich Lutzmann to design the first Opel automobile in 1898.

Opel is from Germany.

P IS FOR PIAGGIO

Piaggio was founded in 1884 and initially produced locomotives and railway carriages.

Today, it is one of the leading world manufacturers of 2-wheeled motor vehicles, including the popular Vespa.

Piaggio is from Italy.

Q IS FOR QOROS

Qoros Automotive Company Limited was founded in 2007. The company's first production model, the Qoros 3 Sedan, debuted in 2013.

An invented word, "Qoros" is meant to evoke the Greek chorus as a reflection of the multi-national nature of the company.

Qoros is from China.

PAGES 36-37

R IS FOR ROLLS-ROYCE

Rolls-Royce was established in 1904 as a partnership between Lord Charles Stewart Rolls and Sir Frederick Henry Royce.

The first Rolls-Royce car, the Rolls-Royce 10hp, was inspired by a Decauville automobile owned by Royce which he succeeded in making significantly quieter than existing cars.

Rolls-Royce is from England.

S IS FOR STUDEBAKER

Founded in 1852, Studebaker was initially a coach-maker, manufacturing wagons, buggies, carriages and harnesses. They began making cars in 1902.

Studebaker's "Lazy S" logo was designed by Raymond Loewy and was used from 1964-1966.

Studebaker is from the USA.

PAGES 40-41

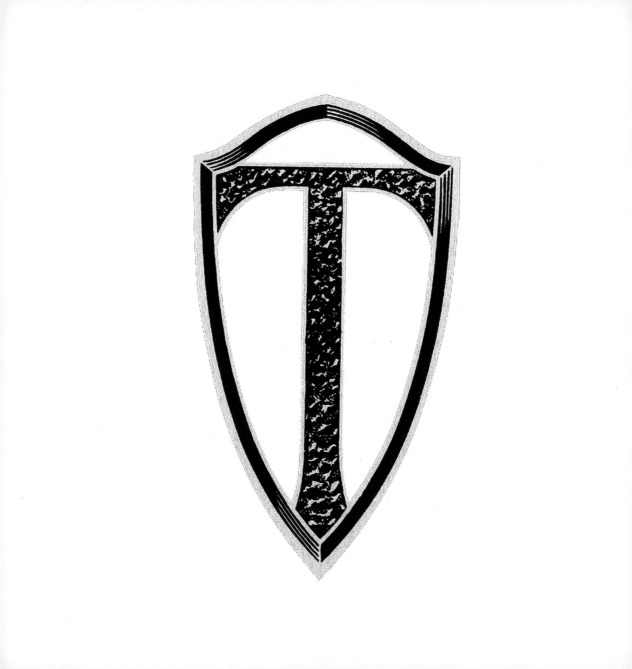

T IS FOR TUCKER

Founded by Preston Tucker, the Tucker Corporation designed cars in Michigan and built them in Chicago in a vast factory that is now the site of the Ford City Mall.

Only 51 examples were made before the company folded on March 3, 1949, amid allegations of fraud.

Tucker is from the USA.

PAGES 42-43

U IS FOR UNIMOG

The Unimog is a range of multi-purpose four-wheel drive medium trucks produced by Mercedes-Benz.

The name Unimog is an acronym for the German "Universal-Motor-Gerät", Gerät being the German word for machine or device.

Unimog is from Germany.

V IS FOR VOLTRA

Voltra Electric revealed an electric car concept in 1963 in three styles: a coupe, a station wagon, and a pick-up truck. Powered by a General Electric traction motor with four heavy-duty batteries, the cars could be recharged at home with a 50-foot self-winding cord.

Unfortunately, the car failed to succeed as it did not receive significant interest from the American public.

Voltra is from the USA.

W IS FOR WOLSELEY

While working for the Wolseley Sheep Shearing Co. in 1895, Herbert Austin designed a car for the company as a way to enter the motor business. The result was a tricar fitted with a flat-twin engine.

Once the largest motor manufacturer in Britain, the company over-expanded, and the Wolseley name lapsed in 1975.

Wolseley is from England.

PAGES 48-49

X IS FOR X by AMC

The 1971 AMC Gremlin X came with mag wheels and tape-stripes borrowed from the Javelin for a sportier look than the original Gremlin.

American Motors Corporation (AMC) was an American automobile company formed by the 1954 merger of Nash-Kelvinator Corporation and Hudson Motor Car Co.

AMC is from the USA.

Y IS FOR YUGO

The first Yugo prototype was manufactured in 1980 by Zastava, a company founded as an arms manufacturer in 1853.

Once the pride of communist Yugoslavia's automobile industry, the last Yugo rolled off its Serbian production line in 2008.

Yugo is from Yugoslavia.

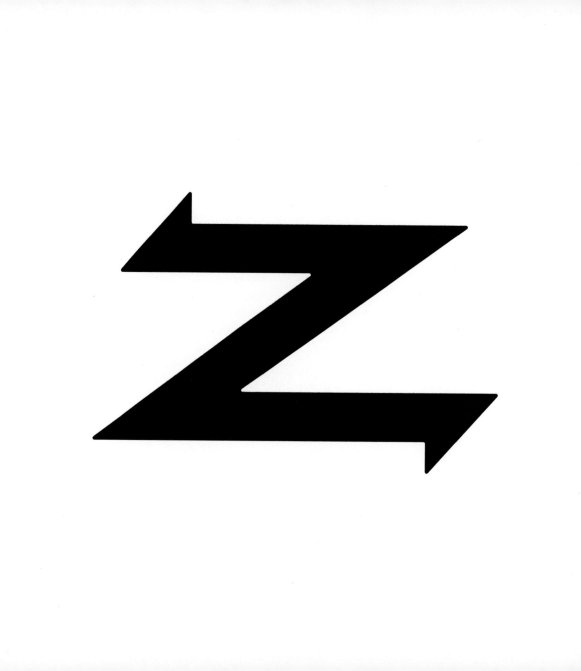

Z IS FOR ZAGATO

Zagato was established in Milan in 1919 by Ugo Zagato.

Zagato's cars were advanced in design and became synonymous with light weight and excellent aerodynamics.

Zagato is from Italy.

LCCN: 2023902594
ISBN: 978-1-951963-17-0

Printed and bound in China
First printing, 2023

+ INFORMATION:
For additional information
on our books and prints,
visit trope.com

CARLOS SEGURA, founder of the Chicago-based design firm Segura Inc., came to the United States from Cuba at the age of nine. The founder of Segura Inc. and the T26 Digital Type Foundry, he previously worked for ad agencies including BBDO, Marsteller, Foote Cone & Belding, Young & Rubicam, Ketchum, and DDB Needham. Segura Inc. and T26 have received numerous awards from organizations around the world, including the 2017 AIGA Fellowship Award, Red Dot, Tokyo Type Directors Club, The Society of Typographic Arts, the New York Art Directors Club, the New York Type Directors Club, and the American Center for Design. Segura's work has been shown in journals including *Graphis*, *Archive*, *Print*, *Communication Arts*, *HOW*, as well as in publications by Taschen, Slanted, PIE Books, Duncan Baird Publishing, F&W Publications, Die Gestalten Verlag Publishing, and others. His work has been shown in exhibits from the Denver Art Museum to Tokyo, Japan, he was named one of the 21st century's 100 best designers by Taschen's 2003 annual "GRAPHIC DESIGN FOR THE 21st CENTURY", was featured in the "Design 50: Who Shapes Chicago" in 2013 and 2014, and was awarded the AIGA Fellowship in 2017. In 2004, he again ventured into a new category when he launched Cartype.com—a creative archive of the automotive industry.